Great Explorers

The Great Polar Adventure

The Journeys of Roald Amundsen

Andrew Langley

Illustrated by Kevin Barnes

Chelsea Juniors
A division of Chelsea House Publishers

Great Explorers
Discovering the New World
Exploring the Pacific
The Great Polar Adventure
Journey into Space

This edition published by Chelsea House Publishers, a
division of Main Line Book Co., 300 Park Avenue South,
New York, New York 10010, by arrangement with
Irwin Jorvik Ltd.

© 1994 Irwin Jorvik Ltd

© 1994 Chelsea House Publishers

1 3 5 7 9 8 6 4 2

ISBN 0-7910-2820-8

Contents

Child of the Snow

Try to remember the coldest, snowiest day you've ever known. The wind is howling; snow is blowing into your face. Now pretend that it is –22°F (-30°C) or colder and you are traveling across a snowfield. You have over 310 miles (500 km) to go and there are mountains and deep crevasses to cross. You are tired, cold, and hungry but you must press on because your goal is the South Pole, probably the most desolate and uninviting place in the world, and you want to be the first person to get there.

It had always been Roald Amundsen's dream to explore the polar regions. He was born in 1872 and as a child in Norway he had been thrilled by the tales of polar explorers. By the time he was 14, Amundsen's mind was made up. He would follow in their footsteps. He trained hard, skiing on the mountains near his home and making long treks through the forests.

In 1894 he made his first voyage to the Arctic on a seal-hunting ship. Three years later he joined an expedition to the Antarctic. But this journey was a disaster. The expedition's ship, the *Belgica,* was frozen in the ice for nearly a year. Many of the crew died and some went mad. Amundsen learned firsthand the dangers of polar exploration.

DID YOU KNOW?

Seal hunting in the Arctic has gone on for hundreds of years. Seals were hunted for their fur, meat, and blubber, the fat that keeps them warm and that was used as a source of oil by the hunters.

DID YOU KNOW?

Fridtjof Nansen was one of the greatest polar explorers of all time. As well as trekking across Greenland, in 1893 he also got nearer to the North Pole than anyone before him. His ship *Fram* was specially designed to be lifted by pack ice and not crushed by it. In this way he was able to drift close to the Pole. He then tried to trek there using dogsleds and kayaks but was turned back by bad weather.

The Last Wildernesses

Why should anyone want to go to the polar regions? They are the coldest places on Earth, covered all the time with snow and ice. Summers are very short, and winters are long and dark.

All the same, many people have gone there. The Inuit (Eskimo) peoples have lived in the Arctic for thousands of years. They hunted the seal, caribou, and other animals, and fished in the seas. Later came the Vikings from Norway, who settled in Greenland.

In the 1500s, many expeditions from northern Europe came to the Arctic. They were searching for a sea route to the north of America that would take them to Asia. All they found were ice and a jumble of bays and islands.

Explorers in the far south were also stopped by ice. James Cook was the first European to sail over the Antarctic Circle in 1773, and in 1841 James Ross came face to face with the Great Ice Barrier.

By the beginning of the 1900s, there was a new reason for going to the Poles. Most of the world had been explored, and the Arctic and Antarctic were among the last great unknown regions. Many wanted to be the first to stand at the ends of the earth. The race to the Poles was on.

DID YOU KNOW?

The **aurora borealis** was one of the many spectacular sights that the early Arctic explorers encountered. Also called the Northern Lights, the aurora borealis is a brilliant light show in the sky. In Antarctica it is called the aurora australis.

DID YOU KNOW?

A **Northwest Passage** across the seas of North America had been sought by explorers and traders since the 16th century. They were looking for a quick route from Europe to the silk and spice trading areas of Asia. What they found was a hazardous nightmare of treacherous waters and gigantic icebergs. Many died without finding the passage. Even though a route has now been found, few ships use it because it is too slow and expensive.

North Pole

South Pole

Learning from the Inuit

In June 1903, a little boat named *Gjoa* slipped out of Oslo. On board were Amundsen and five others. It was Amundsen's first great adventure as leader. He was determined to find the Northwest Passage through the Arctic seas. The first stop was Greenland, where Amundsen picked up a team of dogs to pull his sleds. Then he sailed on across Baffin Bay, heading westward.

Threading its way through the ice floes and narrow channels, *Gjoa* reached King William Island. But soon the sea began to freeze all around the ship and the expedition was stuck tight in the ice for the winter. Temperatures dropped to -44°F (-42°C) but Amundsen didn't complain. He set about learning the skills that were to make him a great polar explorer. He made friends with the local Inuit. They taught him to hunt, to drive dogsleds, and to build igloos. Most important of all, they taught him how to stay warm. Inuit clothes were made of reindeer fur and were warm but light.

After a stay of nearly two years, the expedition sailed again in 1905. They completed their journey through the Northwest Passage and landed safely in Alaska. Amundsen set off on skis to the nearest settlement to take the news of his triumph to the outside world.

DID YOU KNOW?

The **Inuit** (also called Eskimos), have lived in the Arctic region for many thousands of years. They crossed from Asia to America about 6,000 years ago and now live in Canada, Alaska, Greenland, and Siberia. They used to live only by hunting and fishing. Many still do, but others live more like other Canadians, Siberians, and Americans.

THE NORTHWEST PASSAGE

Arctic Ocean

Devon Isla

Amundsen Gulf

ALASKA (USA)

Victoria Island

King
William
Island

Arctic Circle

Change of Plan

Amundsen had made the first voyage through the Northwest Passage, but this success only made him bolder still. Now he wanted to be the first person to reach the North Pole. Amundsen's plan was copied from his hero, Nansen. He would sail to the Arctic and become frozen in the ice. Then he would drift with the ice until he got near the Pole.

He made his preparations with great care. He borrowed Nansen's ship *Fram* and chose an experienced crew. Special sleds and skis were built, and warm Inuit clothes were made. Amundsen bought 100 huskies to pull the sleds.

Then he read some shocking news. Two Americans, Cook and Peary, claimed that they had reached the North Pole. Amundsen was beaten before he had even started! Immediately, he changed his plans. He would go to Antarctica instead and be the first one to reach the South Pole.

Amundsen kept his new destination a secret. When the *Fram* left Norway in August 1910, the crew thought they were heading for the Arctic. After four weeks at sea, Amundsen at last told them that they were going south.

After a happy and busy voyage, the *Fram* reached Antarctica early in 1911. Amundsen landed on the Great Ice Barrier and set up camp to prepare for the long, cold winter months.

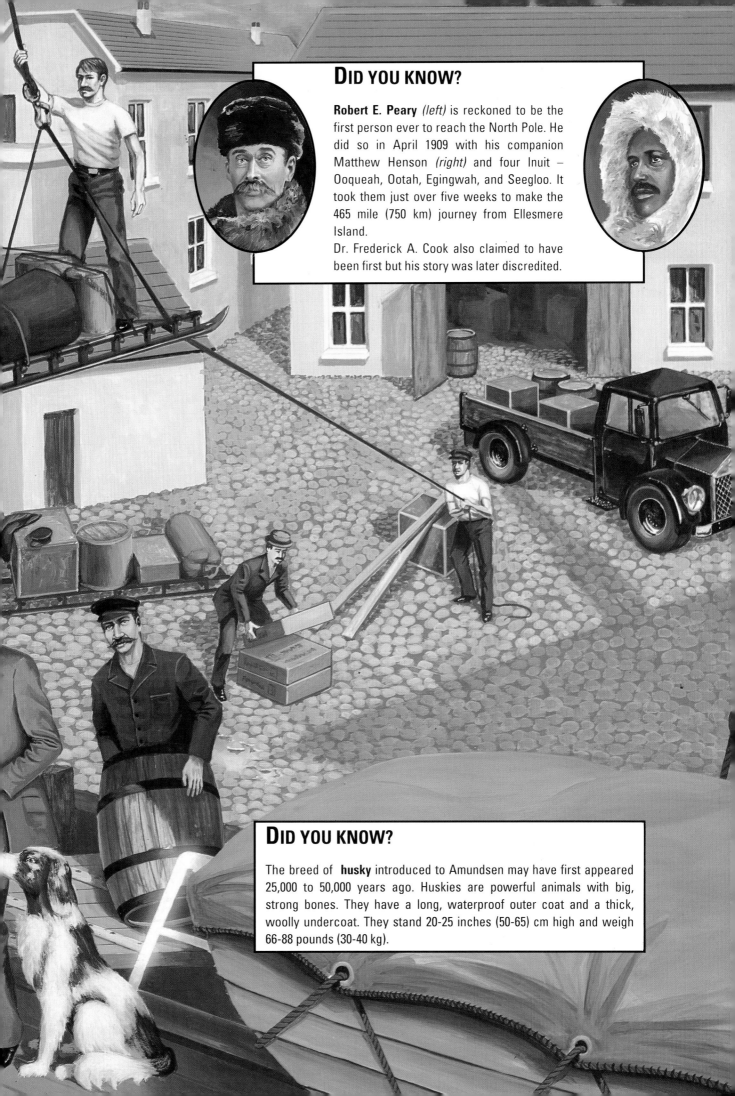

DID YOU KNOW?

Robert E. Peary *(left)* is reckoned to be the first person ever to reach the North Pole. He did so in April 1909 with his companion Matthew Henson *(right)* and four Inuit – Ooqueah, Ootah, Egingwah, and Seegloo. It took them just over five weeks to make the 465 mile (750 km) journey from Ellesmere Island.

Dr. Frederick A. Cook also claimed to have been first but his story was later discredited.

DID YOU KNOW?

The breed of **husky** introduced to Amundsen may have first appeared 25,000 to 50,000 years ago. Huskies are powerful animals with big, strong bones. They have a long, waterproof outer coat and a thick, woolly undercoat. They stand 20-25 inches (50-65) cm high and weigh 66-88 pounds (30-40 kg).

Antarctic Night

Amundsen was delighted to find that the Antarctic snow was ideal for skiing. The dogs, too, worked well. They pulled the sleds carrying equipment from the *Fram* to the base camp.

Here the crew built snug living quarters and stored all their supplies. Spaces for workshops were dug into the snow around the camp. The dogs lived in tents nearby. Amundsen then began to prepare for the final part of the journey. He and his men set up depots at regular intervals on the route to the South Pole. They left supplies of food and fuel at these depots, carefully marked with flags.

Then the Antarctic winter began. There was no sun, and it was impossible to travel far. Blizzards raged and temperatures fell to ‑40°F (‑40°C). Soon the encampment was almost completely buried in snow. Inside, everyone worked hard packing sleds and mending equipment, waiting for winter to end.

Amundsen was secretly worried. He knew that he was not the only person trying to reach the Pole. Not far away was a British expedition, led by Captain Robert F. Scott. They had few dogs, but they had ponies and motorized sleds. Would they win the race?

At last, the winter ended and the sun returned. It was time to set out for the South.

DID YOU KNOW?

The **polar seasons** are different from seasons anywhere else on Earth. In the Arctic, midwinter falls in December and in the Antarctic it falls in June. In the polar summer it is light all day, but in the winter it is dark all day and very, very cold. In fact, the coldest temperature ever recorded, −127°F (−89.2°C), was on August 24, 1960, in Antarctica.

DID YOU KNOW?

The **food** that Amundsen took with him was crucial to his success. He knew that he and his men needed fresh meat (from the seals they hunted), wholemeal biscuits, fruit preserves, and "hot cakes" baked from oatmeal. These provided all the vitamins, fiber, protein, and minerals that the men needed for their trek across the polar ice.

Travel on the Ice

Amundsen chose four other men to go with him to the Pole. They took four loaded sleds, each pulled by a team of huskies. The sleds were made mostly of wood, lashed together at the joints. One sled carried the compass to show the way. Another was fitted with a sled meter – a wheel that measured how far they traveled.

Everyone had two pairs of skis in case one broke. They were very long, so there was less danger of falling into crevasses. All the equipment had to be made as light as possible. The wooden runners on the sleds were planed very thin. So were the cases that held the food and fuel. These had special lids that could be opened without untying the ropes.

The food was carefully measured out each day. They ate pemmican (dried beef) mixed with oats and peas, as well as biscuits and milk. They also had fresh seal meat, which had been stored at the depots.

Amundsen and his men wore the light, warm clothes of the Inuit. They were made of reindeer skin and wolfskin. On their feet were three pairs of fur and woolen socks and leather boots stuffed with soft grass.

DID YOU KNOW?

Crevasses are deep cracks in the ice. They can be as wide as 65 feet (20 m), as much as 146 feet (45 m) deep and several hundred feet long. Crevasses are sometimes covered by snow and hidden from view, until someone steps into one.

The Journey South

The expedition set off on October 20, 1911. It was very cold and misty, and the wind blew fiercely, but the men and dogs moved easily over the snow. After a long winter they were eager to stretch their legs.

Fogs and blizzards made it hard to see the way. They got lost several times, and one sled nearly fell into a crevasse. All the same, they safely reached their food depots. "We are going like greyhounds," wrote Amundsen in his diary.

Amundsen was still worried that Captain Scott would reach the Pole before him. He could not know that Scott had only just begun, and was over 186 miles (300 km) behind the Norwegians.

By the middle of November the expedition came to its biggest obstacle – a glacier, a huge frozen river, full of crevasses and chunks of ice. Somehow they climbed it and trekked through a massive range of mountains.

Amundsen had now reached the high ground of the Antarctic Plateau. Still the going was very hard. They had to fight their way through blizzards and across a sheet of smooth, slippery ice, which they called "the Devil's Ballroom." Then at last the going became easier, and they sped on toward the Pole.

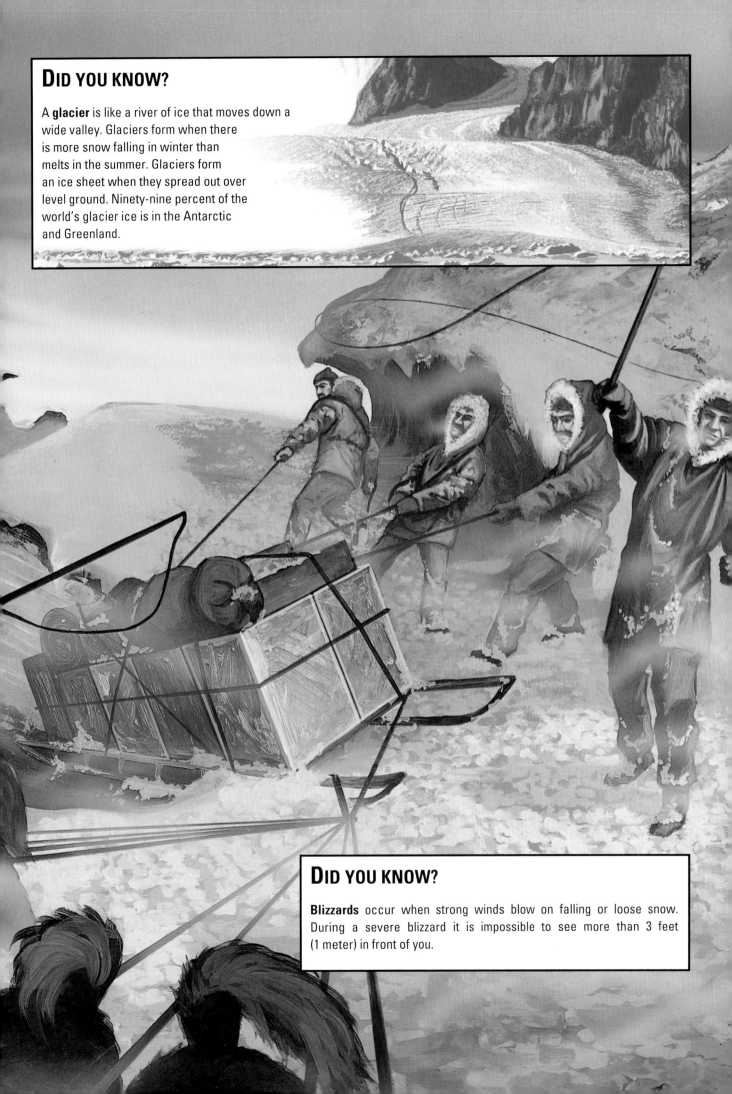

DID YOU KNOW?

A **glacier** is like a river of ice that moves down a wide valley. Glaciers form when there is more snow falling in winter than melts in the summer. Glaciers form an ice sheet when they spread out over level ground. Ninety-nine percent of the world's glacier ice is in the Antarctic and Greenland.

DID YOU KNOW?

Blizzards occur when strong winds blow on falling or loose snow. During a severe blizzard it is impossible to see more than 3 feet (1 meter) in front of you.

At the Pole

AMUNDSEN

Amundsen drove men and dogs onward. They kept up a steady pace of 15 miles (24 km) each day. By the evening of December 13, the party was exactly that distance from the South Pole.

The next day was clear and bright. They raced on, with Amundsen in the lead. All at once, shouts went up. The sled meter showed that they had reached their goal. They peered about carefully, but there was no sign of the British expedition. Scott was still a long way behind, and traveling much more slowly. Amundsen had won the race!

Together the five men planted a Norwegian flag in the snow. They spent the next three days making sure that they really were at the Pole. They took measurements from the sun and covered a wide area. Then they set off on their return journey. "Farewell, dear Pole," wrote Amundsen, "I don't think we'll meet again." He left behind a spare tent with some clothes and a note to greet Captain Scott.

But Scott did not arrive at the Pole until over a month later. It was a terrible blow to him to see that he had been beaten. Still worse he was running short of food, and his men were weak and ill. Amundsen, meanwhile, was returning to the safety of his base camp near the coast.

BJAALAND

HANSSEN

HASSEL

WISTING

South Pole Dec. 14, 1911

Last depot Dec. 8

Main depot Nov. 17
Depot Nov. 16

Depot Nov. 29
Depot Nov. 21

84° depot Nov. 13

83° depot Nov. 9

82° depot Nov. 4

81° depot Oct. 31

80° depot Oct. 23

Fram
Heim
Bay
of Whales

Ross Sea

The Winner and the Loser

The race was not over yet. Amundsen still had to be the first to get the news of his triumph to the outside world. He and his men traveled faster than ever. The wind was behind them, and they now had only two sleds. Amundsen had planned the whole journey so well that they had plenty of food and fuel. They picked up more supplies at each depot.

Soon they reached the mountains and the glacier again. They lost their way, but then found their old path. This time they could ski down the frozen river at high speed. In a few hours they were at the bottom. Amundsen pushed on. They now had more food than they needed. On January 26, 1912, they arrived back at base camp, all fit and well. Only four days later, the *Fram* sailed away from Antarctica for the last time. Amundsen made straight for Hobart, Tasmania, where he sent out telegrams telling of his success.

Back in Antarctica, Scott and his men were still trudging through ice and snow. Their ponies had died and they had to pull their own equipment. They were running out of food and knew that Amundsen had beaten them to the Pole. Very soon they were all dead.

DID YOU KNOW?

Icebergs are a constant hazard for ships in polar seas. They are formed when giant pieces of ice break off the ice shelf. Usually about four-fifths of an iceberg is hidden under the water. One of the largest, formed in 1963, measured 68 by 47 miles (110 by 75 km).

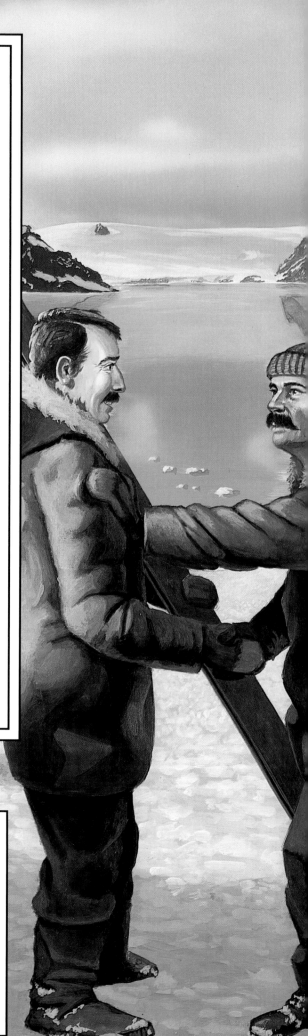

Did you know?

Wildlife is abundant in the seas around Antarctica. The tiniest of all is plankton. This is eaten by small shrimplike creatures, called krill, which are, in turn, eaten by penguins and other birds, squid, fish, seals, and baleen whales. Birds and seals rarely venture inland. Those that do usually die from cold and hunger. However, that same cold can preserve their bodies. Some specimens 3,000 years old have been found.

Humpback whale

Emperor penguin

Arctic tern

Krill

Back to the Arctic

Amundsen became famous throughout the world. But he had two big problems. How was he to pay off the enormous debts he had built up? And what was he to do next? He raised money by giving lectures in Europe and America. Then he went back to what he liked doing best – exploring the Arctic.

Amundsen sailed from Oslo again in June 1918. He had a new ship, *Maud,* and with him came many of his old companions from the *Fram.* They followed the coast of Siberia, heading east. Winter came, and the *Maud* was frozen in the ice. Here luck turned against Amundsen. He broke his arm and was attacked by a polar bear. It was not until 1921 that he completed his voyage into the northern Pacific.

Amundsen knew that the old days of dogsledding were over. Aircraft were a much quicker and easier way of traveling over the ice. In 1925, he tried to fly to the North Pole but failed. A year later he flew right across the Arctic Circle, this time in an airship.

In 1928, Amundsen set out on one last adventure. He took off in an aircraft to find a pilot who had crashed on the Arctic ice. But Amundsen's plane also crashed, and he was never seen again. He died in the ice and snow where he had spent so much of his life.

24

DID YOU KNOW?

The **polar bear** is one of the largest of the bear family. Polar bears have keen eyesight and a sharp sense of smell. Some scientists think that polar bears can smell seals and meat from 12 miles (20 km away).

Poles Under Threat

When Amundsen died, the race for the North and South poles was long over. But vast areas of Antarctica and the Arctic were still unexplored. Over the next fifty years, travelers and scientists tried to fill in the gaps. The Canadians and Russians sent expeditions to explore the islands of the Arctic and to find out the depth of the sea there. In 1944, Henry Larsen sailed a Canadian ship through the Northwest Passage and back again, opening the way for cargo ships.

Aircraft and snow tractors now made ice travel much easier. Many people attempted to cross the Antarctic from sea to sea. In 1958 a British expedition, led by Vivian Fuchs, traveled across Antarctica in only 99 days. Dogs were still sometimes used. In 1969, Wally Herbert used dogsleds when he led the first party to cross the whole surface of the Arctic ice.

Meanwhile, many countries of the world had come to stake their claims on the polar lands. Expeditions from Australia, France, Scandinavia, and Russia explored parts of the Antarctic continent. The Americans built five military and scientific bases there. In 1958, twelve nations shared in the building of 55 research stations.

Not all these expeditions have been careful in their treatment of the environment, and today both the Arctic and Antarctic are in danger of being seriously damaged by humans.

Some scientists at the poles want to test nuclear bombs there. The seas have been plundered for whales and fish. Pollution may cause the earth to heat up, melting ice and bringing great changes to the environment. The future for the Arctic and Antarctic is far from safe.

The Legacy of Amundsen

The expeditions of Amundsen and other polar explorers and scientists have had more positive effects, too. We have learned much about Antarctica and the animals that live on its shores and in its seas. Fossil plants found there tell us that the continent was once much warmer than it is now, while rock samples suggest that Antarctica was once joined to South America and Africa.

We have learned how important the region is in shaping the weather around the world and, because the atmosphere around Antarctica is still quite clean, it is a good place for scientists to make studies of world pollution, the greenhouse effect, and the hole in the ozone layer.

American scientists have searched the Antarctic for meteors, studied why fish blood does not freeze, and investigated how deep seals and penguins dive beneath the ice. French scientists are studying deep layers of ice to find out how much more polluted the earth is now compared to hundreds of years ago.

Nowadays polar scientists live much more comfortably than Amundsen and his team. They use motorized sleds, their laboratories are heated, and they have high-technology equipment and radios to keep in touch with the outside world. But they never forget the pioneering work of men like Roald Amundsen who opened up the polar regions for scientists and made their modern research possible.

DID YOU KNOW?

Ozone is an invisible layer of gas in the earth's atmosphere. It protects us from certain harmful rays of the sun. Recently, scientists in Antarctica have noticed that the ozone layer over that continent is getting thinner. If this "ozone hole" gets bigger the sun's rays could threaten people, plants, and animals.

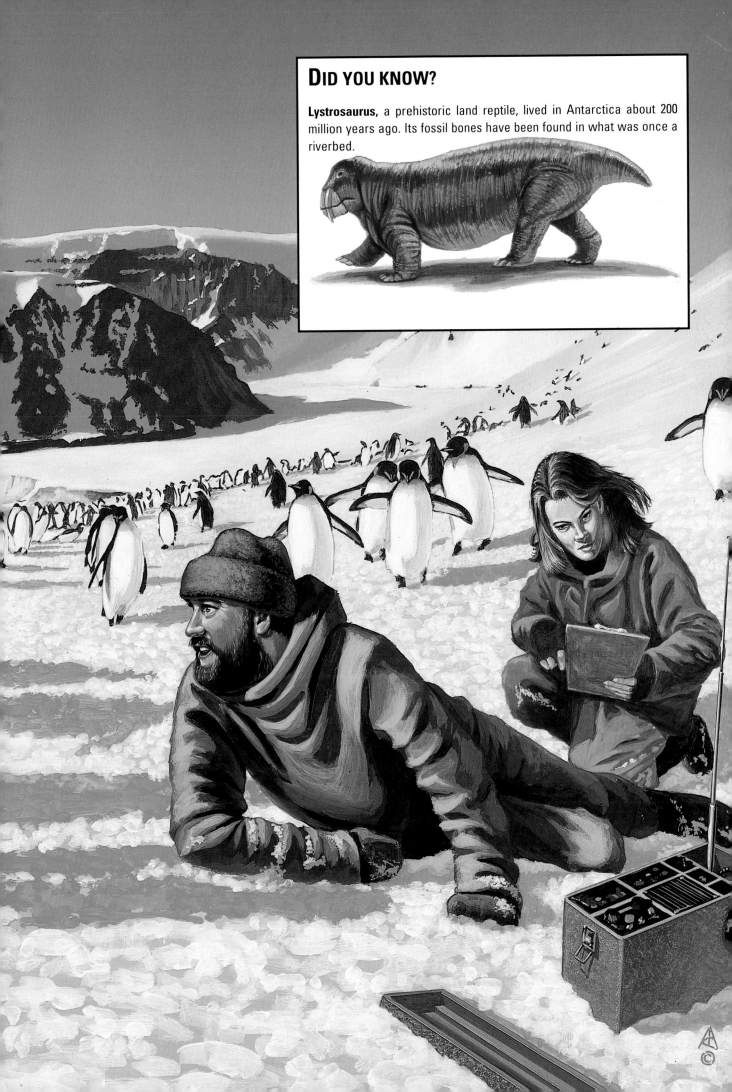

DID YOU KNOW?

Lystrosaurus, a prehistoric land reptile, lived in Antarctica about 200 million years ago. Its fossil bones have been found in what was once a riverbed.

Glossary

Arctic and Antarctic circles Imaginary circles drawn around the earth, marking off the polar regions from the warmer areas to the north and south.

Fiber A tough substance found in some foods. It helps the stomach to digest.

Great Ice Barrier (also called **Ross Ice Shelf**) The sheer ice cliffs that form part of the coast of Antarctica.

Greenhouse effect When pollution in the atmosphere causes the sun's heat to be trapped near the earth. This heats up the earth like the soil in a greenhouse.

Ice floe A large, flat sheet of ice that forms a crust over the sea in very cold places.

Igloo An Inuit home or hunting camp made from blocks of ice.

Kayak An Inuit canoe.

Plankton Very tiny plants and animals that float in the sea.

Protein A substance found in many foods. It helps build muscles.

Vitamins A number of substances found in many foods. They help keep you healthy and free from diseases.